HI-TECH JOBS WITHOUT COLLEGE

BE A DIGITAL MARKETER

by Sue Bradford Edwards

BrightPoint Press

San Diego, CA

BrightPoint Press

an imprint of ReferencePoint Press, Inc.
Printed in the United States

For more information, contact:
BrightPoint Press
PO Box 27779
San Diego, CA 92198
www.BrightPointPress.com

LIBRARY OF CONGRESS CATALOGING-IN-PUBLICATION DATA

Name: Edwards, Sue Bradford, author.
Title: Be a digital marketer / by Sue Bradford Edwards.
Description: San Diego, CA: ReferencePoint Press, 2026 | Series: Hi-tech jobs without college | Includes bibliographical references and index. | Audience: Grades 7–9
Identifiers: ISBN 9781678212667 (hardcover) | ISBN 9781678212674 (eBook)
The complete Library of Congress record is available at www.loc.gov.

CONTENTS

AT A GLANCE

- Digital marketers are advertisers. They help people find out about products and services.
- The digital world is where people see much of today's advertising. The average American spends about 7 hours online each day.
- Digital marketing can be blog posts or websites. It can be videos or even emails.
- Algorithms are sets of rules and guidelines that a computer program follows. They affect what each person sees online, including which ads they see.
- Digital marketers work with search engine optimization (SEO). This includes using key words and structuring content to achieve higher rankings in searches.

- A college degree is not necessary for someone to become a digital marketer. Some people in this field earn certifications or are self-taught.

- An online portfolio can help a job candidate show off their skills. This is important if they have no experience in the field.

- Artificial intelligence (AI) tools can help digital marketers work more quickly.

A DIGITAL MARKETER'S DAY

People see Neil Patel's work every day. He is a digital marketer. His company, NP Digital, advertises for big companies such as Levi's and CNN. NP Digital's ads appear on TikTok and Facebook. The company also builds websites. Patel and his team help companies reach their customers.

Patel often works from home. In the morning, he does research. He notices

Digital marketers spend part of each day online, researching which types of ads audiences are responding to.

which ads are getting a lot of clicks. Each afternoon, he creates social media content. This might mean blog posts or videos. He makes sixteen videos each month. These videos appear on the NP Digital

Drawing out ideas for ads or videos can help digital marketers plan and visualize how finished products might look.

YouTube channel. Patel shows people how to create digital marketing ads. Some viewers contact Patel's company. They become clients. They pay NP Digital to market their companies. The videos Patel makes are a form of digital marketing themselves. They promote NP Digital's services to potential clients.

A lot of work goes into Patel's videos. First, he brainstorms ideas. He gets some ideas by talking to other marketers. He studies the types of videos people are sharing. He makes a list of his ideas.

Next, he creates a storyboard. This is a plan or map for the video. It looks like a graphic novel. It lists each scene and has a sketch of what the viewer will see. It includes action, dialogue, and graphics.

Patel spends about 8 hours outlining and writing his scripts.

Finally, Patel films the videos. He or a team member edits the videos. Then someone uploads them to the company's YouTube channel.

WHAT DOES A DIGITAL MARKETER DO?

Digital marketers are advertisers. Companies such as NP Digital help other companies get the word out about their products. First, they research their **target market**. This helps marketers create content that customers will interact with. The data also shows which sites customers visit. Patel and his team post videos or ads where customers will see them.

Marketers gather facts, figures, and other forms of data to learn about their target audiences.

Digital marketers then create content. They make videos and ads to promote a product. They also build websites. This is where they tell the story of the company. They create posts that appear on social media and in apps. Digital marketers interact with customers. Millions of people online see their work each day.

EXPLORING DIGITAL MARKETING

Every day, the average American spends about 7 hours online. They view online content using their phones, computers, tablets, and TVs. People see ads when they read emails and watch videos. They see ads when they use search engines. More ads pop up when they play games or visit social media sites. They see ads whenever they are online.

Americans spend a lot of free time online, making them a major audience for digital marketers.

YouTuber Benaminute wanted to know how many ads he saw in one day. As he read emails, he counted ads. He counted ads on Facebook and other sites. His total was 692. Later, he went to a professional football game. He lost count at 3,000 ads in 3 hours.

Digital marketers create digital ads and videos. They create emails that encourage people to buy products. These are just a few types of digital marketing.

CREATING DIGITAL MARKETING

Digital marketing can be very effective. This is because digital marketers have access to data. Laurie Wang was a digital marketer at Google. She explains why data is important. Through digital ads, marketers can track who is seeing the ads. They can see where customers view the ads. They are also able to tell who buys a product after seeing an ad. This means that the customers are responding to the content. This is called audience engagement.

The average person sees many ads each day but remembers only a small portion of them.

Digital marketers use this data to learn which types of ads sell more products. They also use it to learn which site or app customers are using. This data allows marketers to target ads to the right audience.

Wang explains that companies also need a website. Digital marketers help clients build engaging websites. The goal is to create **brand awareness**.

Websites are where businesses tell their stories. Websites explain what companies do. They describe why their product is important. This helps turn site visitors into customers.

A good website is key to digital marketing. Wang says, "This is the one asset that you currently do own."[1] The

Gathering information about a company's target audience is key to successful digital marketing.

website will be there whenever customers search for it. In contrast, some ads are temporary. They can be hard to find again.

Social media marketing is also important. These are ads or videos posted on sites such as Facebook or Instagram. A company might place ads on YouTube, X, or TikTok. Data helps digital marketers find the best **platforms** for their audience.

Marketers also seek out influencers. Influencers create posts and videos about

With the help of social media influencers, digital marketers can increase brand awareness for their products.

a specific topic. They build a community of followers. Companies may ask influencers to talk about their products.

Michelle Bali was a creative strategist at Shopify. It was her job to think of ways to market products. One of Bali's clients was Jenna Meek, the founder of the beauty brand Shrine. Bali paired Meek with influencer and British model Jess Hunt. Hunt had a big following on Instagram. She posted videos about how to apply natural-looking makeup. Together, Meek and Hunt launched the makeup line REFY. Hunt posted videos about REFY products to promote them.

Bali explains what it takes to work with an influencer. "You don't need to pay influencers to endorse your products," says Bali. "There are hundreds of thousands of influencers [who] would be willing to do it for free."[2]

An influencer helps information about a product reach a larger audience. But not everyone on a social media platform sees every post. What each user sees is controlled by algorithms.

ALGORITHMS

An algorithm is a set of instructions. On social media, they determine what users see in their feeds. Posts that rise to the top have more likes or clicks. Or they may match content the user has responded to before. Google uses an algorithm to rank pages and sites in a search.

For example, a person may search for a brand of camping gear. Google's algorithm looks for camping gear sites. It puts those with the most activity at the top of the search. Search engine result pages contain ads. A platform called Google Ads selects these ads. Some will be for competing brands. Others will be for local stores that sell camping gear. Perhaps the user has searched for canoes before. They may see ads for canoeing and camping.

Google is always changing its algorithm. This helps to prevent advertisers from **manipulating** the algorithm. One way advertisers do this is by overusing keywords. A camping site might use the

Writing for Computers

Computer programs are written using programming languages. People use these languages to write code, or instructions that computers can follow. Code tells the computer what to do. Algorithms may be translated into code. Learning to write and read code can help digital marketers improve websites. It can also help them **automate** tasks.

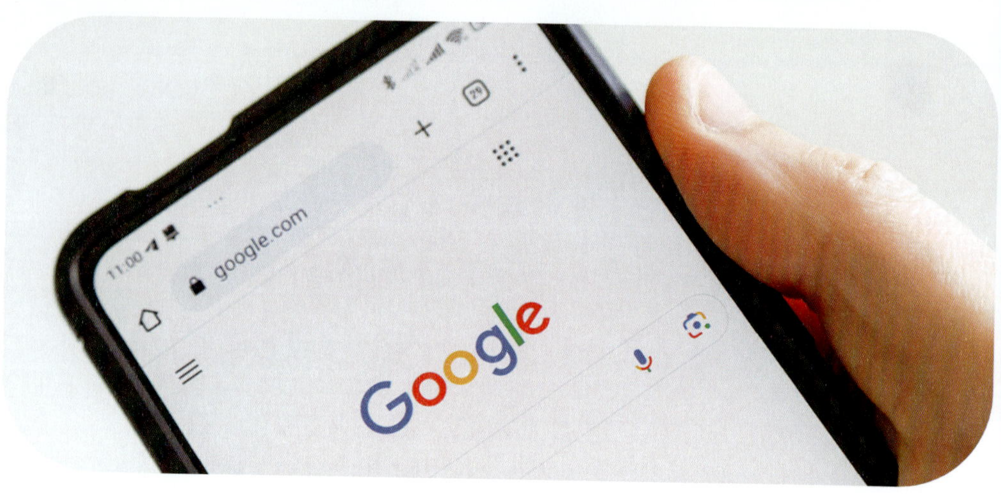

Google uses an algorithm to determine what appears first in online searches.

word *camping* repeatedly. Or it might include the names of competing brands.

Digital marketers try to figure out how algorithms work. Then they structure their website or ad to get the highest search ranking. Including product details is important. They use keywords in the ad. These include the price of an item. The location of the business can also be helpful. Vague promises do not help. Saying "the best tent ever" will drop the ad in the list of results.

THE LATEST TECH

Just as algorithms change, what technology can do changes, too. How digital marketers use technology is always evolving. Digital marketers use artificial intelligence (AI). This is software that enables a computer to do tasks usually done by humans. AI gathers data about how people learn, make choices, and solve problems.

AI helps digital marketers see what customers are buying. For example, more people may begin to buy a certain brand of athletic shoe. AI may see a pattern. The same people who buy the shoes also buy glow-in-the-dark laces. The marketers may add "Customers who buy this shoe also buy these laces" to the webpage.

Virtual reality can be a way for marketers to show potential customers the benefits of a product or experience.

Digital marketers are also using augmented reality (AR). In AR, an app can be used to bring digital content into the viewer's real-world location. The furniture store IKEA has used AR. Customers could download the IKEA Place app. Using the app, they could select a desk from IKEA's site. Then they could turn on the camera.

This allowed them to see what the desk looked like in their room.

Virtual reality (VR) is similar to AR. The main difference is that in VR, a computer program creates a location. For example, a digital marketer may want to promote a new gym. They could create a virtual model of the gym. People could wear a headset to take a tour. They might see the basketball courts. They could see a skateboard park. They could even read the snack bar menu. Seeing the space in this way can help sell gym memberships.

Digital marketers do many different tasks. They must like working with technology. Creativity and problem-solving skills help, too. There are a few different ways to learn how to be a digital marketer.

TRAINING FOR DIGITAL MARKETING

Digital marketers need several skills. First, they must know how to gather and use data. Digital marketers work with a lot of data. They need to learn about the customers they are trying to engage. This includes finding out which sites customers visit. Knowing which social media platforms and apps they use is helpful, too. Marketers also gather data about the products customers are buying.

Gathering as much data as possible allows digital marketers to make informed decisions about the best ways to engage customers.

Digital marketers must also understand search engine optimization (SEO). When a person looks for something online, they type in a word or question. Search engines such as Google and Bing look for related keywords. Digital marketers must know how and when to use keywords to sell products. SEO includes using keywords on websites, ads, or blog posts. But SEO also involves how content is structured. Marketers need to know where to place these words on a website. It's important to place these words where the search engine will find them.

Good copywriting skills are important, too. This means writing text that convinces customers to take action. That action could be buying products. Or it could be paying for services. Digital marketers use

Writing convincing copy can mean using stories from customers who were happy with a product.

copywriting to create social media posts or websites. The writing must grab the reader's attention. It also has to be clear.

FORMAL EDUCATION

Some digital marketers get college degrees. But they are not needed. People can learn these skills at boot camps. They can also earn digital marketing certificates.

A boot camp is a fast and focused program. Digital marketers can learn the skills they need quickly. There are many boot camps. The JobPrepped Digital Marketing Boot Camp is only 12 weeks long. Classes focus on digital marketing. People study analytics. They learn about paid ads and working with influencers. Boot camps offer an intense experience.

Another option is a certificate program. Students must pass a test to earn a digital marketing certificate. The University of Missouri offers a certificate in digital marketing. Students study online for 10 weeks. They learn to use AI and SEO. They study social media marketing and email marketing. When finished, they get a certificate from the university.

Coursera is an online learning platform. It offers Google's Digital Marketing and

At in-person and online training programs, digital marketers learn how to use and analyze data.

E-Commerce certificate. Learners can sample the program during a free 7-day trial. Students take eight classes. They learn about e-commerce or online sales. They learn how to interact with customers as professionals. They also learn about email marketing.

SELF-TAUGHT

Some people teach themselves digital marketing. Nicole Quinones did this after she set up an online store. "My **entrepreneurial** spirit led me to dive into the e-commerce world. In the process, I wore many hats and learned valuable skills along the way," Quinones says.[3]

Quinones did everything herself. She wrote product descriptions. She took

Soft Skills

Not every digital marketing skill is learned in class. Soft skills are behaviors. They affect how someone works with people. A good digital marketer is curious. They ask questions. They have empathy. They understand how people think. They are also a good communicator. They make things easy to understand.

pictures of her products. She filled orders. It was a lot of work. But it helped her learn how to run a business. Sometimes she made mistakes. But eventually she learned what worked best for her business. She searched online. She found a lot of information in forums. She talked to her customers to learn what they wanted.

THE ONLINE PORTFOLIO

Many companies ask to see examples of a digital marketer's work. A portfolio website can help with this. It is an online space that shows off a person's best work. It can show off marketing videos. It can also link to a website built for a client. A portfolio can briefly describe a person's job experience. It is a great way to show off a person's skills.

Creating a thoughtful portfolio of work can be key to getting a job in digital marketing.

Having a portfolio is important for those new to digital marketing. They may not have digital marketing job experience. But the portfolio shows what they can do.

A portfolio website starts with a home page. It also has a contact page. This includes an email address or a phone number. Other pages feature the person's projects.

Kamillah Rae is a new digital marketer. She got a job with no experience. She believes her portfolio was the key. "You're still just a drop in a pool of resumes that all look the same. This is when a portfolio website can swoop in and be your secret weapon," she says.[4]

Rae tells recent students to focus on the job they want. The portfolio should include only examples that relate to that job. If they have no experience, they should be creative. An online portfolio can show off web design and coding skills.

Edward Wood is the head of marketing at CareerFoundry. This is an online school. It focuses on helping people learn technical skills. He interviews a lot of job candidates. He says only 20 percent of digital marketing **applicants** include a portfolio. Applicants who do have an advantage. He can see what they are able to do.

Wood explains that a portfolio should tell him about a candidate's digital marketing experience. The home page should also list their skills. These might include training in SEO. Or it could be making videos. It should list the tools they've used. These might include programs, apps, or computer languages.

The projects are the main part of the portfolio. Wood says that work samples demonstrate skills. Projects should also include proof points. These are data showing how many people have read a post and added a comment. A statement from a client is a proof point, too. Proof points show that a person's work is effective. With solid training, job candidates will soon be working as digital marketers.

Portfolios should include hard data that shows a digital marketing ad was effective.

WORKING IN DIGITAL MARKETING

A digital marketer's daily tasks vary. Often, what they do depends on where they work. Someone who works at an **agency** does projects for many different clients. Someone who works for one company focuses on one brand.

Some digital marketers freelance. Companies and clients pay them to handle digital marketing tasks. They often work in their home office. Good communication

Digital marketers study online ads to learn what their audience likes.

The ability to work on a team is an important skill for digital marketers.

skills are important. Freelancers need to ask questions about what the client wants. They also need to be able to explain ad results in a way clients will understand.

TEAMWORK

Many digital marketers may work together as a team. Each person works on a different marketing task. One may plan email **campaigns**. Another works on the SEO for the company website. Team members must communicate often. This helps keep projects on schedule.

NP Digital is a global company. Team members live and work in the United States, Malaysia, Mexico, and other countries. The company has more than 900 clients. Neil Patel stays in touch using email. This is how he communicates with teammates and clients. He answers up to 1,000 emails each day.

COLLECTING DATA

Some people think digital marketing is as easy as posting on social media. But there's a lot more to it than that. Becky Giannelli teaches digital marketing. She says, "You'll soon realize that very few people outside the world of digital marketing know exactly what it is that you do."[5]

One of a digital marketer's main tasks is to learn which ads are working and which aren't. To do this, they must study data. A web service called Google Analytics can help.

The service gathers information about site visitors. It counts how many visitors come to a site. It notes how much time each visitor spends there. And it keeps track of the bounce rate. This is when someone lands on a page and then leaves. They don't click through to other pages on the site. Google Analytics also tracks conversions. A conversion is when ads and media posts have the desired outcome. This might mean the person bought the product in the ad. Or they may have signed up for a class.

When early posts in a campaign perform poorly, a digital marketer makes changes. Reels might replace longer videos. TikTok might become the focus instead of Facebook.

Digital marketers spend time each day tracking audience engagement and news about the economy.

Video editing can be a key skill for digital marketers, as videos make up a good amount of online content.

THE ECONOMY

Patel doesn't stop with this kind of data. He also checks the daily news. He reviews stock prices on Google. This helps him see how the economy is doing. World events affect his global business.

Global events can impact a marketing campaign for jeans such as Levi's.

Hurricanes mean ships cannot bring in cargo. The jeans are stuck onboard. When people cannot get what they order, the campaign can fail. To save it, digital marketers may change their message. They may decide to make customers think the jeans are worth the wait.

Celebrities can also have a global impact. In 2024, Beyoncé released her song "Levii's Jeans." The popularity of denim clothing went up 14 percent. Digital marketers created Levi's ads using her song in the background.

CONTENT CREATION

Many digital marketers create content. This content could be videos, blog posts, or podcasts. It could be newsletters or email campaigns. These campaigns often require that multiple emails be written and sent.

Before digital marketers create content, they come up with a goal. This could be to inform customers about a new product. Or it could be for half of the email list to open the newsletter.

After a goal is set, digital marketers brainstorm ideas and create content. Roy Furr is a content creator. He helps businesses grow. He recommends having a set plan for content creation. The plan might be to create enough videos in one day to post throughout a month. He says it is easy to spend hours making one video. But with the goal of making a month of content, a person spends the same time making a batch of videos. With a focused goal, people work more efficiently.

Making more content in less time may mean giving some tasks to other people. "Outsource elements of the process that make sense for you to outsource," says Furr.[6] For example, Furr makes his content, but he outsources publication. His assistant posts the videos on YouTube.

What's New

Digital marketing is always changing. New social media platforms are launched. Algorithms change. The types of posts people like change, too. Digital marketers find out about all of this and more in newsletters. Industry newsletters include *HubSpot*, *Simplilearn*, and *Search Engine Land*. Digital marketers also read *Marketo*, *DigitalMarketer*, and *Social Media Examiner*.

READ AND RESPOND

Digital marketers check their company's social media feeds often. Likes are important. But comments and direct messages (DMs) are more important.

It's the job of someone on the digital marketing team to read and respond to comments. DMs also require attention. A customer might say she likes her new tent. The digital marketer could thank her. The digital marketer could also ask her to post a review. A customer might complain that a shoe isn't available in red. The digital marketer could direct that customer to a red shoe that the company sells.

Responses let customers know someone is listening. This builds community. And it helps create more sales. Customers are

Digital marketers do many different jobs. Here are some job titles sorted by skills.

more likely to do business with companies that listen to them. Digital marketers do more than look after customers. They also look to the future.

CHAPTER FOUR

LOOKING AHEAD

The Bureau of Labor Statistics collects information on US jobs. It states that marketing will grow by 8 percent between 2023 and 2033. In 2023, 411,300 people worked in marketing. By 2033, 442,400 people will work in marketing.

The outlook for digital marketing is bright. Online Marketing Institute noted that companies want to hire digital marketers. They need people who specialize in

SEO is an area that is changing all the time, requiring digital marketers to stay current on the latest advancements.

SEO, website development, and social media marketing.

AI-BASED FUTURE

AI is used in many social media tools. Apps powered by AI can help digital marketers save time. AI Chat helps marketers write posts. StoryChief is social media management software. It creates posts and helps choose strong SEO terms.

FeedHive helps produce new content quickly. It uses AI to recycle old posts. Digital marketers then reshape content based on current trends.

Buffer is a program that schedules content. Posts can be scheduled on several different platforms. AI reviews a scheduled post. It alters the text to best fit where it will be posted. Buffer also gathers data about the gender, age, and location of customers.

ContentStudio tracks information by topic. It shows how well an individual post is doing. This helps digital marketers see which platforms their audience is using. For example, is the audience still on X, or have users moved to Bluesky?

In early 2025, mobile-first indexing was changing SEO development. This means search engines used a site's mobile device content to set its ranking.

CONTENT

AI isn't the only thing that's changing how digital marketers work. Customers want to hear from real people. They want more than just to see an ad telling them the tent is good. They want another person's opinion.

Because of this, many digital marketers are turning to the company's employees. A digital marketer can record a video of an employee for Instagram. The employee might talk about their job. Or maybe the employee describes a camping trip they took with their family. Employees give a company personality.

"This type of content is very popular because it showcases very relatable people. . . . This allows for more . . . stories to be told from behind the scenes of the brand," says Alison Battisby.[7] Battisby is the founder of Avocado Social. It helps businesses connect with their audience on social media.

Digital marketers can encourage customer-created content. Amazon does this when it asks people to post a video review of a product. This creates community. Customers hear from

Privacy

Countries around the world are passing new privacy laws. Europe's General Data Protection Regulation is one such law. These laws govern how companies gather information about their customers. Customers must be told when information is being collected. Privacy laws are changing the information available to digital marketers.

Five-star reviews sell products. About 94 percent of consumers state that reviews and online ratings help them decide which products to buy.

each other. They share what they like. They provide solutions to problems.

GENERATION ALPHA

Digital marketers must learn about new customers. Generation Alpha includes those born between 2010 and 2025. Members of this generation value buying used or second-hand items. This means they may buy fewer luxury items.

Jim Lecinski teaches marketing. He points out that Generation Alpha has grown up using technology. He says:

> *I'm not sure an Instagram post is going to be sufficient. I think [there are] different ways that we have to engage them, touching on our social values and allowing them to engage with a community digitally.*[8]

Generation Alpha will soon be entering the workforce. They will make jobs like digital marketing their own. The work they do will reflect their values. It will also highlight the values of their customers.

GLOSSARY

agency

a business that offers a service such as marketing to a variety of other companies

applicants

people who are applying for a job

automate

to do tasks automatically

brand awareness

recognizing a company, its products, or its services

campaigns

marketing plans for products that can include posts, videos, and emails

entrepreneurial

associated with creating and developing a business

platforms

digital spaces where users interact, post content, and view posts

target market

a specific group of customers who are the focus of a product or service

SOURCE NOTES

CHAPTER ONE: EXPLORING DIGITAL MARKETING

1. Laurie Wang, "Digital Marketing 101—A Complete Beginner's Guide to Marketing (Explainer Video)," *YouTube*, uploaded by Laurie Wang, June 2, 2023. www.youtube.com.

2. Quoted in "Influencer Marketing Tutorial: Go from Beginner to Pro in 20 Minutes," *YouTube*, uploaded by Learn with Spotify, September 11, 2023. www.youtube.com.

CHAPTER TWO: TRAINING FOR DIGITAL MARKETING

3. Nicole Quinones, "Fun Facts: My Journey in Self-Taught Digital Marketing," *LinkedIn*, October 27, 2023. www.linkedin.com.

4. Kamillah Rae, "The Portfolio Website that Got Me Hired: How to Make an Impressive Portfolio with No Experience," *YouTube*, uploaded by Kamillah Rae, March 5, 2023. www.youtube.com.

CHAPTER THREE: WORKING IN DIGITAL MARKETING

5. Becky Giannelli, "A Juggling Act: A Day in the Life of a Digital Marketer," *Simplilearn*, July 26, 2025. www.simplilearn.com.

6. Roy Furr, "7 Tips to MASSIVE Content Creation: Digital Marketing Content Creation," *YouTube*, uploaded by Roy Furr—Breakthrough Marketing Secrets, March 6, 2023. www.youtube.com.

CHAPTER FOUR: LOOKING AHEAD

7. Quoted in "What Are the Digital Marketing Trends for 2025?" *Digital Marketing Institute*, April 22, 2025. https://digitalmarketinginstitute.com.

8. Quoted in "What Are the Digital Marketing Trends for 2025?"

FOR FURTHER RESEARCH

BOOKS

Tammy Gagne, *Be a Data Analyst*. Brightpoint Press, 2026.

The Young Influencer's Handbook: Build Your Brand, Gain Followers, Secure Sponsorships, and Create Click-Worthy Content. Applesauce Press, 2021.

Andrew Yueh, *JavaScript Coding for Teens: A Beginner's Guide to Developing Websites and Games*. Rockridge Press, 2021.

INTERNET SOURCES

Jitudan Gadhavi, "The Future of High Tech Digital Marketing: Strategies and Considerations," *Sun Media Marketing*, June 20, 2024. www.sunmediamarketing.com.

"Marketing: What Is It and Why Do Companies Need It?" *Coursera*, March 25, 2025. www.coursera.org.

"What Does a Digital Marketer Do?" *Digital Marketing Institute*, August 6, 2024. https://digitalmarketinginstitute.com.

WEBSITES

CMI: The Content Marketing Institute

https://contentmarketinginstitute.com

The Content Marketing Institute is all about online education in content marketing. This site includes articles, e-books, and training about digital marketing.

HubSpot

https://blog.hubspot.com

HubSpot helps businesses land and keep happy customers. Even industry experts come to HubSpot to learn.

Neil Patel

https://neilpatel.com

Neil Patel is a digital marketer. His site offers digital marketing tips, free tools, and more.

INDEX

IMAGE CREDITS

Cover: © Gorodenkoff/Shutterstock Images
5: © Insta_Photos/Shutterstock Images
7: © Constantinis/iStockphoto
8: © deucee_/iStockphoto
11: © ipuwadol/iStockphoto
13: © Jose Calsina/Shutterstock Images
15: © dibrova/Shutterstock Images
17: © Kaspars Grinvalds/Shutterstock Images
18: © PixelVista/iStockphoto
22: © Markus Mainka/Shutterstock Images
24: © Ground Picture/Shutterstock Images
27: © DC Studio/Shutterstock Images
29: © GaudiLab/Shutterstock Images
31: © Chay_Tee/Shutterstock Images
34: © PeopleImages.com-Yuri A./Shutterstock Images
37: © CarlosBarquero/Shutterstock Images
39: © PeopleImages.com-Yuri A./Shutterstock Images
40: © Insta_Photos/Shutterstock Images
43: © MMD Creative/Shutterstock Images
44: © Gorodenkoff/Shutterstock Images
49: © smx12/Shutterstock Images
51: © da-kuk/iStockphoto
53: © Nongasimo/Shutterstock Images
56: © Ken Stocker/Shutterstock Images

ABOUT THE AUTHOR

Sue Bradford Edwards is a nonfiction author who writes about culture, history, and science. She enjoys helping young readers explore possible jobs. Her books include *Become a Construction Equipment Operator, Life as an Army Ranger, and 10 Ways to Use a Degree in Computer Science.*